Lire à petits pas Niveau

Méthode Montessori pour apprendre à lire : du mot au livre

French English German Spanish - Romanian

fire

feu

Feu

fuego

foc

Fire is hot.

---

car

voiture

voiture

coche

mașină

My car is fast

---

horse

cheval

cheval

caballo

cal

The horse is galloping.

boat   bateau

bateau

barco   barcă

The boat is sailing.

---

ground   sol

sol

suelo   sol

It plays a trick on the ground.

---

window   fenêtre

fenêtre

ventana   fereastră

The window is open.

paper

papier

papier

papel

hârtie

I like to color on paper.

hoe

houe

houe

azada

sapă

Use a hoe in the garden.

fish

poisson

poisson

pez

peşte

There are two fish.

cat

chat

chat

gato

pisică

That cat is adorable.

picture

image

image

imagen

imagine

He is taking some pictures.

face

visage

visage

cara

față

They were at the face painting booth.

water   l'eau

l'eau

agua   apă

He is drinking water.

---

floor   sol

sol

suelo   podea

The girl sits on the floor.

---

day   journée

journée

día   zi

This day is the 30th.

rose

rose

Rose

rosa

Trandafir

Thank you for the rose.

feet

pieds

pieds

pies

picioare

His feet are swollen.

sun

soleil

Soleil

dom

 soare

The sun is very bright.

hill   colline

colline

colina   deal

The house is on the hill.

France   france

France

francia   Franţa

Have you ever been to France?

---

letter   alphabet

alphabet

alfabeto   alfabet

Learn English letters is fun.

chicken
poulet
poulet
pollo
pui
The chicken is laying eggs.

street
rue
rue
calle
stradă
They walk across the street.

top
haut
Haut
tapas
top
We like to play with tops.

place · endroit

endroit

sitio · loc

This is my favorite place.

cotton · coton

coton

algodón · bumbac

A q-tip is made of cotton.

city · ville

ville

ciudad · oraș

He worked in the city.

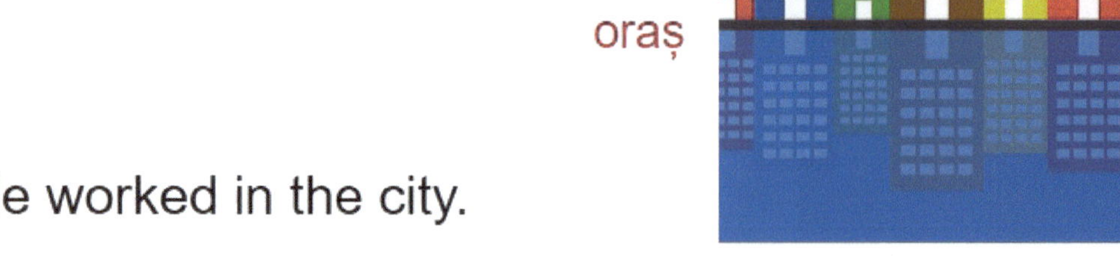

flower   fleur

fleur

flor   floare

She is holding a flower.

robin   robin

Robin

robin   prihor

The robin is helping Santa.

baby   bébé

bébé

bebé   bebelus

The baby is crawling.

bread   pain

pain

un pan   pâine

She is baking some bread.

---

seed   la graine

la graine

semilla   sămânță

We will plant the seeds.

---

man   homme

homme

hombre   om

This man is my dad.

rabbit	lapin

lapin

conejo	iepure

The rabbit wants to play.

time	temps

temps

hora	timp

He is telling the time.

Greek	grec

grec

griego	greacă

Have you ever had Greek food?

family

famille

familia

famille

familie

famille

How big is your family?

children

les enfants

niños

les enfants

copii

les enfants

Four children sang.

brother

frère

hermano

frère

frate

frère

They are brothers.

corn   blé

blé

maíz   porumb

I grow corn in the garden.

---

mother   mère

mère

madre   mamă

My mother loves me.

---

conditions   conditions

conditions

condiciones   condiţii

What are the weather conditions.

school   école

école

colegio   şcoală

They are going to school.

---

coat   manteau

manteau

saco   palton

She is wearing her coat.

---

morning   matin

Matin

mañana   dimineaţă

I wake up in the morning.

father   père

père

papá   tata

He is a nice father.

---

sister   sœur

sœur

hermana   soră

She is my sister.

---

milk   lait

Lait

leche   lapte

The baby is drinking milk.

oxygen

oxygène

oxygène

oxígeno

oxigen

What is the symbol for oxygen?

O₂

---

four

quatre

quatre

cuatro

patru

There were four of them.

---

children

les enfants

les enfants

niños

copii

The children are playing.

grass   herbe

herbe

césped   iarbă

The goat is eating the grass.

---

apple   pomme

Pomme

manzana   măr

Apples are a popular fruit.

---

name   nom

Nom

nombre   Nume

My name is Joe.

home   maison

maison

casa   Acasă

He drew a picture of his home.

---

bear   ours

ours

oso   urs

The bear likes to eat honey.

---

leg   jambe

jambe

pierna   picior

My leg is feeling better.

duck   canard

canard

pato   rață

The duck is swimming.

game   jeu

Jeu

juegos   jocuri

What game is it?

wind   vent

vent

viento   vânt

The wind blows the leaves.

box   boîte

boîte

caja   cutie

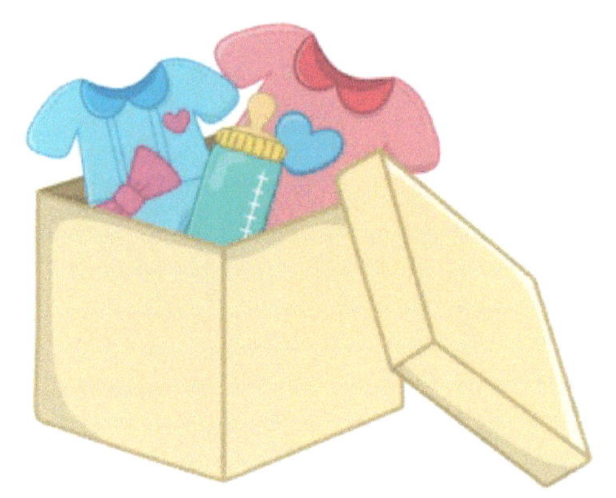

The box is full of clothes.

---

ball   balle

Balle

pelota   minge

He is bouncing the ball.

---

chair   chaises

chaises

sillas   scaune

He is sitting on the chair.

toy — jouet

jouet

juguete — jucărie

He has a whole box of toys.

shoe — chaussure

chaussure

zapato — pantof

I have new shoes.

way — façon

façon

camino — cale

They find a way back home.

watch   l'horloge

l'horloge

reloj   ceas

My watch is ticking.

---

cake   gâteau

gâteau

pastel   tort

The cake is white and pink.

---

chart   graphique

graphique

gráfico   diagramă

What does your medical chart say?

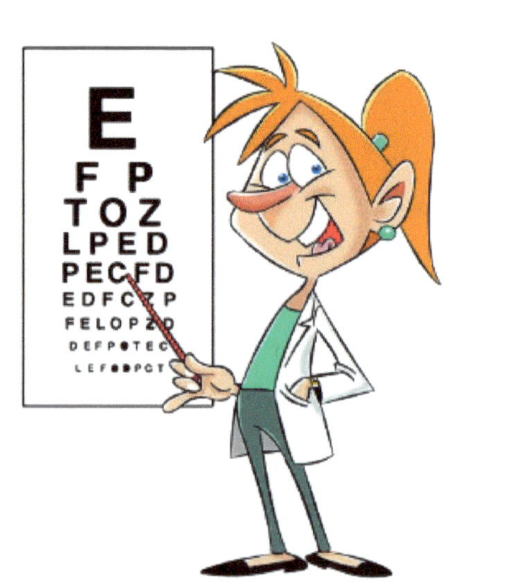

seat   siège

siège

asiento   scaun

The girls took a seat in the sand.

---

fresh   frais

Frais

fresco   proaspăt

All the fruit is fresh.

---

money   argent

argent

dinero   bani

I save money in my piggy bank.

rain	pluie

pluie

lluvia	ploaie

We love the rain!

---

dog	chien

chien

perro	câine

The dog wants to eat sweets.

---

boy	garçon

garçon

chico	băiat

The boy is eating dinner.

page

page

page

página

page

pagină

Please turn the page.

cloche

bell

cloche

campana

cloche

clopot

I hear the bell ringing!

chose

thing

chose

cosa

chose

lucru

I am thinking of many things.

song   chanson

chanson

canciones   cântece

She is singing a song.

---

kitty   minou

minou

gatito   Kitty

I like my kitty.

---

eye   œil

œil

ojo   ochi

He is closing his eyes.

<table>
<tr><td>men</td><td>hommes</td></tr>
</table>

Hommes

hombres   bărbați

The men are arguing.

<table>
<tr><td>party</td><td>fête</td></tr>
</table>

fête

fiesta   partid

I love to go to parties.

<table>
<tr><td>snow</td><td>neige</td></tr>
</table>

neige

nieve   zăpadă

I have fun in the snow.

exemple

This is an example of a bird.

poupée

She is hugging her doll.

tête

She has a hat on her head.

bed — lit

lit

cama — pat

We all share three beds.

---

stick — bâton

bâton

palo — băț

He is playing sticks.

---

farm — ferme

ferme

granja — fermă

The farm has lots of animals.

table

table

table

mesa

masa

There is a toy on the table.

---

squirrel

écureuil

écureuil

ardilla

veveriţă

The squirrel is on the tree.

---

garden

jardin

jardin

jardín

grădină

They are going to the garden.

hand   main

main

mano   mână

You should wash your hands.

night   nuit

nuit

noche   noapte

We sleep at night.

gun   pistolet

pistolet

pistola   arme

We played with a water gun.

tree   arbre

arbre

árbol   copac

She is sitting under a tree.

---

sheep   mouton

mouton

oveja   oaie

The sheep have fluffy wool.

---

food   aliments

aliments

comida   alimente

They made a lot of food.

idea idée

idée

idea idee

I have an idea!

---

company compagnie

compagnie

empresa companie

What company do you work for?

---

wood bois

bois

madera lemn

He plays with wooden blocks

church   église

église

iglesia   biserică

Did you go to church?

---

bird   oiseau

oiseau

pájaro   pasăre

The bird is dancing happily.

---

ring   bague

bague

anillo   inel

The bird is holding a ring.

office — bureau

Bureau

oficina — birou

Do you need any office supplies?

---

farmer — fermier

fermier

agricultor — agricultor

The farmer had a farm.

---

rope — corde

corde

cuerda — frânghie

Do you have any rope?

house   maison

maison

casa   casă

We live in the same house.

nest   nid

nid

nido   cuib

The bird has a nest.

egg   oeuf

Oeuf

huevo   ou

The bunny has many eggs.

birthday anniversaire

anniversaire

cumpleaños zi de nastere

Today is my birthday.

---

goodbye au revoir

Au revoir

adiós la revedere

The bear is saying goodbye.

---

girl fille

fille

niña fată

The girl is pretty.

door · porte

porte

puerta · uşă

He is knocking on the door.

---

column · colonne

colonne

columna · coloană

Did you read the newspaper column?

---

nose · nez

nez

nariz · nas

My nose is running.

cow   vache

vache

vaca   vacă

The cow is standing up.

---

score   but

But

puntuación   scor

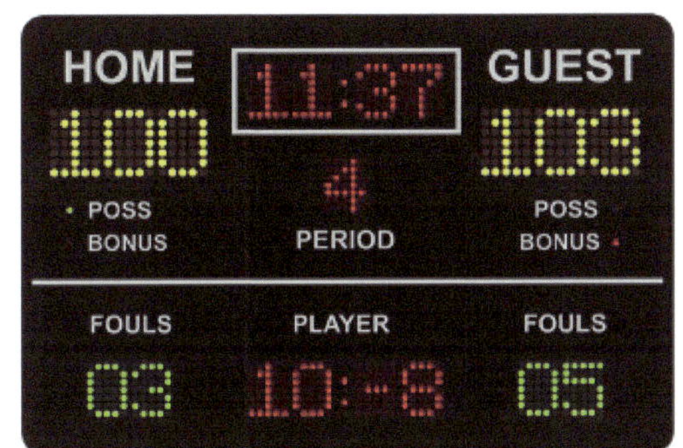

What was the final score?

---

pig   porc

porc

cerdo   porc

She is lying on the pig.